My Favorite Horses

RACEHORSES

Stephanie Turnbull

A⁺
Smart Apple Media

Published by Smart Apple Media,
an imprint of Black Rabbit Books
P.O. Box 3263, Mankato, Minnesota, 56002
www.blackrabbitbooks.com

Designed by Hel James
Edited by Mary-Jane Wilkins

Cataloging-in-Publication Data is available from the Library of Congress

ISBN 978-1-62588-182-3

Photo acknowledgements
l = left, r = right; t = top, b = bottom
title page TongRo Images/Shutterstock; 3 Margo Harrison/
Shutterstock; 4-5 NEIL ROY JOHNSON/Shutterstock; 6, 7, 8 pirita
Shutterstock; 9 jakelv7500/Shutterstock; 11 Neale Cousland/
Shutterstock; 12, 13 Mikhail Pogosov/Shutterstock; 14 Jess Yu/
Shutterstock.com; 15 Mikhail Pogosov/Shutterstock; 16 NEIL ROY
JOHNSON, 17 Perry Correll/both Shutterstock.com; 18 Chris Hellyar/
Shutterstock.com; 19 Dennis Donohue/Shutterstock; 20 Cheryl Ann
Quigley/Shutterstock.com; 21t Featureflash/Shutterstock.com,
b AlexanderZam/Shutterstock.com; 22 David Acosta Allely/
Shutterstock.com; 23 M. Rohana/Shutterstock.com
Cover Margo Harrison/Shutterstock

Printed in China

DAD0055
032014
9 8 7 6 5 4 3 2 1

Contents

Flying Feet 4
Champion Racers 6
Ready to Race 8
Racing Gear 10
And They're Off! 12
Fast and Furious 14
Up and Over 16
Racing Wheels 18
Famous Races 20
Unusual Races 22
Useful Words 24
Index 24

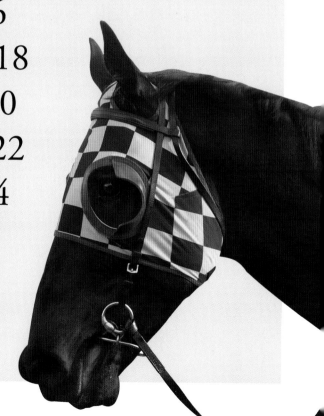

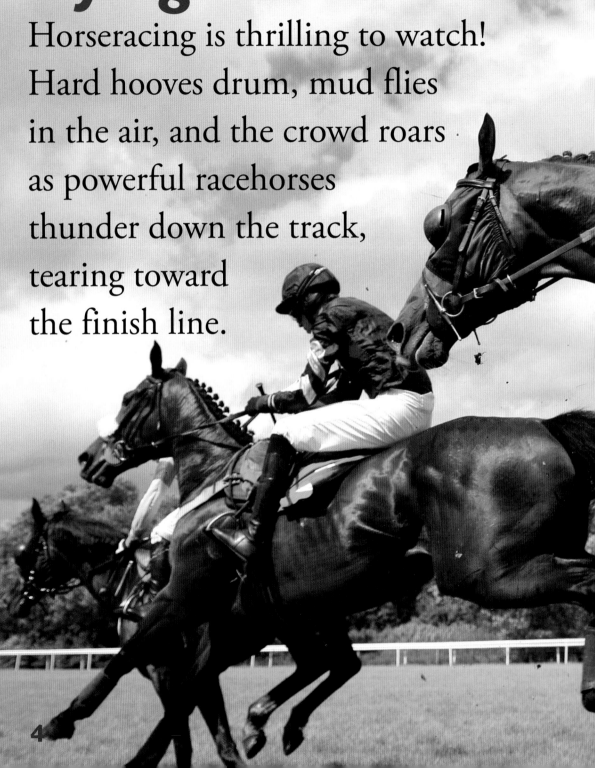

Flying Feet

Horseracing is thrilling to watch!
Hard hooves drum, mud flies
in the air, and the crowd roars
as powerful racehorses
thunder down the track,
tearing toward
the finish line.

Champion Racers

Most racehorses
are Thoroughbreds.

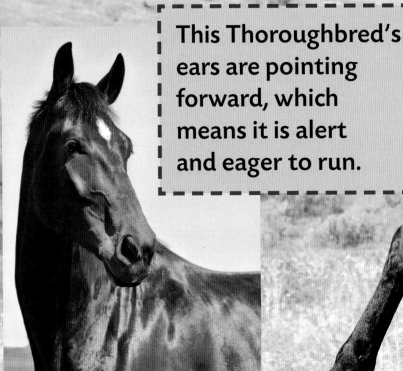

This Thoroughbred's
ears are pointing
forward, which
means it is alert
and eager to run.

Thoroughbred horses
are long-legged, fast,
and full of energy.

Ready to Race

Horses begin training when they are one year old. They learn to carry a rider and gallop next to other horses.

Horses start racing at the age of two. By the time they are three years old, they may be winning top races.

Trainers and vets keep them clean, neat, and healthy.

Racing Gear

Racehorses wear small saddles with high footholds called stirrups. This lets riders perch above the saddle and lean forward.

Riders are called jockeys. They wear colorful hats and shirts called silks. They carry whips, but must use them carefully.

Some horses have eye shields called blinkers to keep them looking straight ahead.

And They're Off!

Before a flat race, trainers lead their horses into boxes called starting stalls. The horses stamp and snort nervously as they wait for the race to begin.

Suddenly the front doors spring open and the horses burst out of the stalls as quickly as they can. The race is on!

Fast and Furious

Flat races can be short sprints or long, tough runs.

Who wins depends on how fit horses are, how easy they find the track to run on, and how well jockeys control them.

Sometimes fast horses carry extra weights to help slower horses catch up. This makes the finish really exciting!

Winners may get trophies and ribbons.

Up and Over

Steeplechases are races
with fences to jump over.

Some fences have water
to splash through
or a deep ditch
to leap across.

Fences are made
with real or
artificial twigs.

Steeplechases can be dangerous. Horses may fall at jumps or throw off their jockey.

Racing Wheels

In harness racing, horses pull riders in tiny, two-wheeled carts called sulkies. Horses have to trot or pace. They must never gallop!

Sturdy Standardbred horses usually run these races.

Riders sit with their legs up and hold on tightly as they race down the track.

Famous Races

Horse races are held all over the world.

The Kentucky Derby is one of the most famous races in the US —even though the race is over in two minutes!

The winning jockey wears a garland of roses.

Guests at grand events such as England's Royal Ascot love to dress up!

The Melbourne Cup is an old, well-known Australian race.

60° REG

Australia

CARBINE 1890
150TH MELBOURNE CUP

Unusual Races

Not all races are run on tracks.

Every year in Sanlúcar, Spain, horses dash across the sand in exciting beach races.

Another famous race
is held in Siena, Italy.
Ten riders in colorful
costumes gallop
bareback around
the main square as
a huge crowd cheers.

Useful Words

gallop The fastest way a horse can run, lifting all four hooves off the ground.

trot A kind of jog, when the horse moves its legs in diagonal pairs.

pace A speedy way of running. A horse moves its left front and back legs together, then its right ones.

whip A long, bendy rod that a jockey swishes against a horse's sides to startle it into going faster.

Index

blinkers 11

flat races 12, 13, 14, 15

galloping 8, 18, 24

harness racing 18, 19

jockeys 10, 14, 15, 17, 20

jumps 16, 17

saddles 10
steeplechases 16, 17
stirrups 10

Thoroughbreds 6, 7
trainers 9, 12
trotting 18, 24

whips 10, 24